W9-CHJ-999

Forensic Scientist

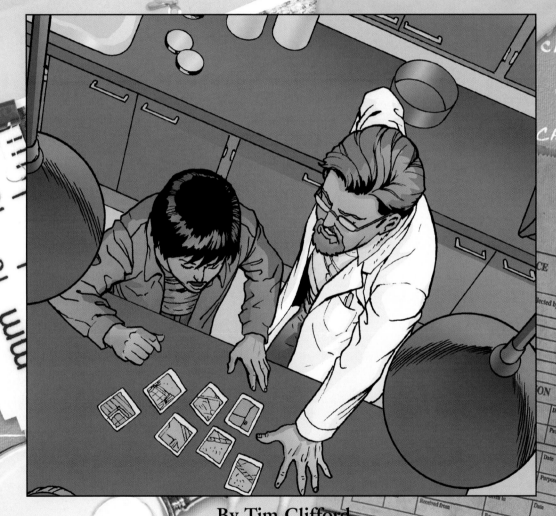

By Tim Clifford
Illustrated By Ken Hooper
Colored By Lance Borde

ROURKE PUBLISHING

Vero Beach, Florida 32964

www.rourkepublishing.com

PHOTO CREDITS: © YuryKhristich: © spxChrome: © alexkz: © Living Images: © NNehring: © ABDesign: Title page and pages 4, 5, 26, 27, 28, 29, 30, 31; © mrloz: page 27; © jangeltun: page 28

Edited by Katherine M. Thal
Illustrated by Ken Hooper
Colored by Lance Borde
Art Direction by Renee Brady
Page Layout by Heather Botto

Library of Congress Cataloging-in-Publication Data

Clifford, Tim, 1959-
 Forensic scientist / Tim Clifford.
   p. cm. -- (Jobs that rock graphic illustrated)
 Includes bibliographical references and index.
 ISBN 978-1-60694-371-7 (alk. paper)
 ISBN 978-1-60694-554-4 (soft cover)
 1. Forensic sciences--Comic books, strips, etc. 2. Forensic
sciences--Juvenile literature. I. Title.
 HV8073.8.C55 2010
 363.25--dc22

                    2009020481

Printed in the USA
CG/CG

www.rourkepublishing.com - rourke@rourkepublishing.com
Post Office Box 643328 Vero Beach, Florida 32964

Table of Contents

Meet the Characters .Page 4

Chapter 1: The Crime . . . . .Page 6

Chapter 2: The Investigation . . . . .Page 10

Chapter 3: The Solution . . . . .Page 22

Discover More . . . . .Page 26

Websites . . . . .Page 29

Glossary . . . . .Page 30

Index . . . . .Page 31

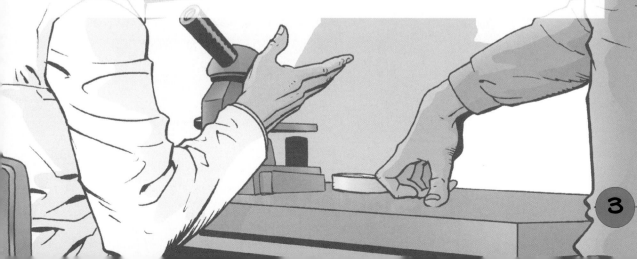

Meet the Characters

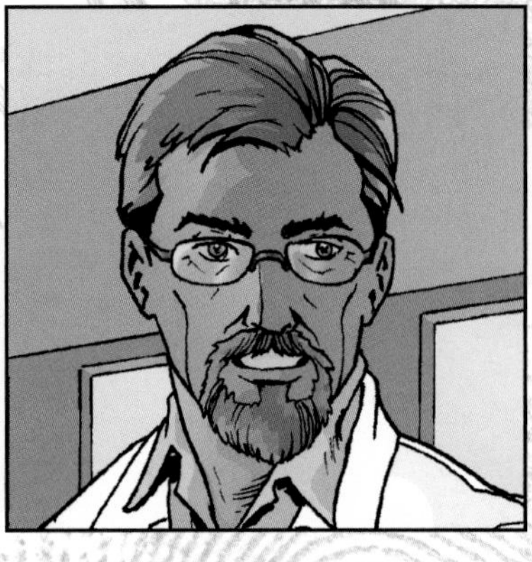

Mr. Vince Dee

Mr. Vince Dee, Calvin and Shelley's dad, is a forensic scientist.

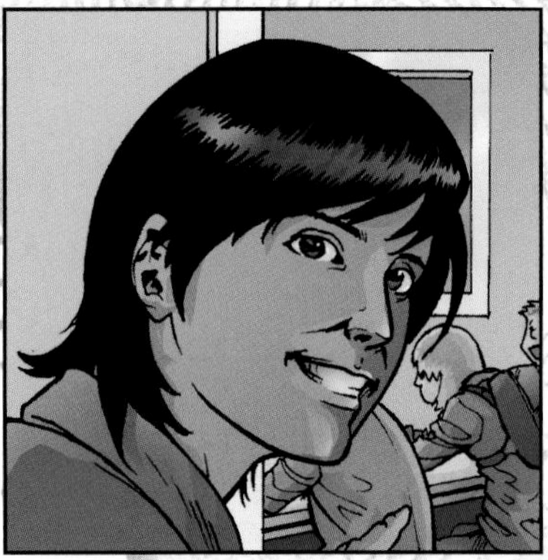

Calvin Dee

Calvin is 12 years old and wants to be a forensic scientist someday.

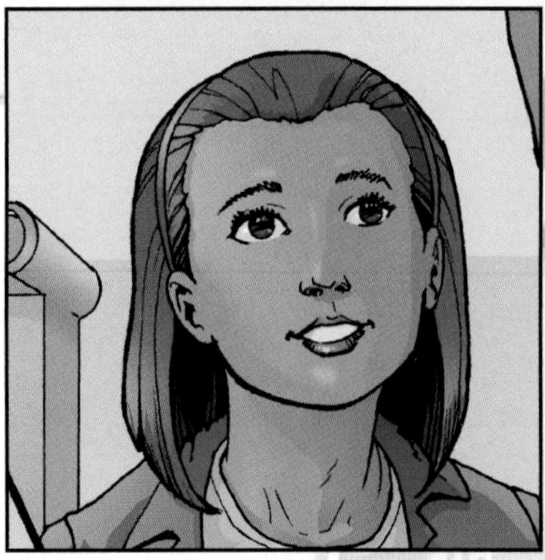

Shelley Dee

Shelley is Calvin's sister and assistant in helping to solve the crime.

Cyclone

Cyclone is the Dee family's dog.

Danny

Danny is 12 years old and Calvin's friend from school.

Todd

Todd is 12 years old and Calvin's friend from school.

Chapter 1: The Crime

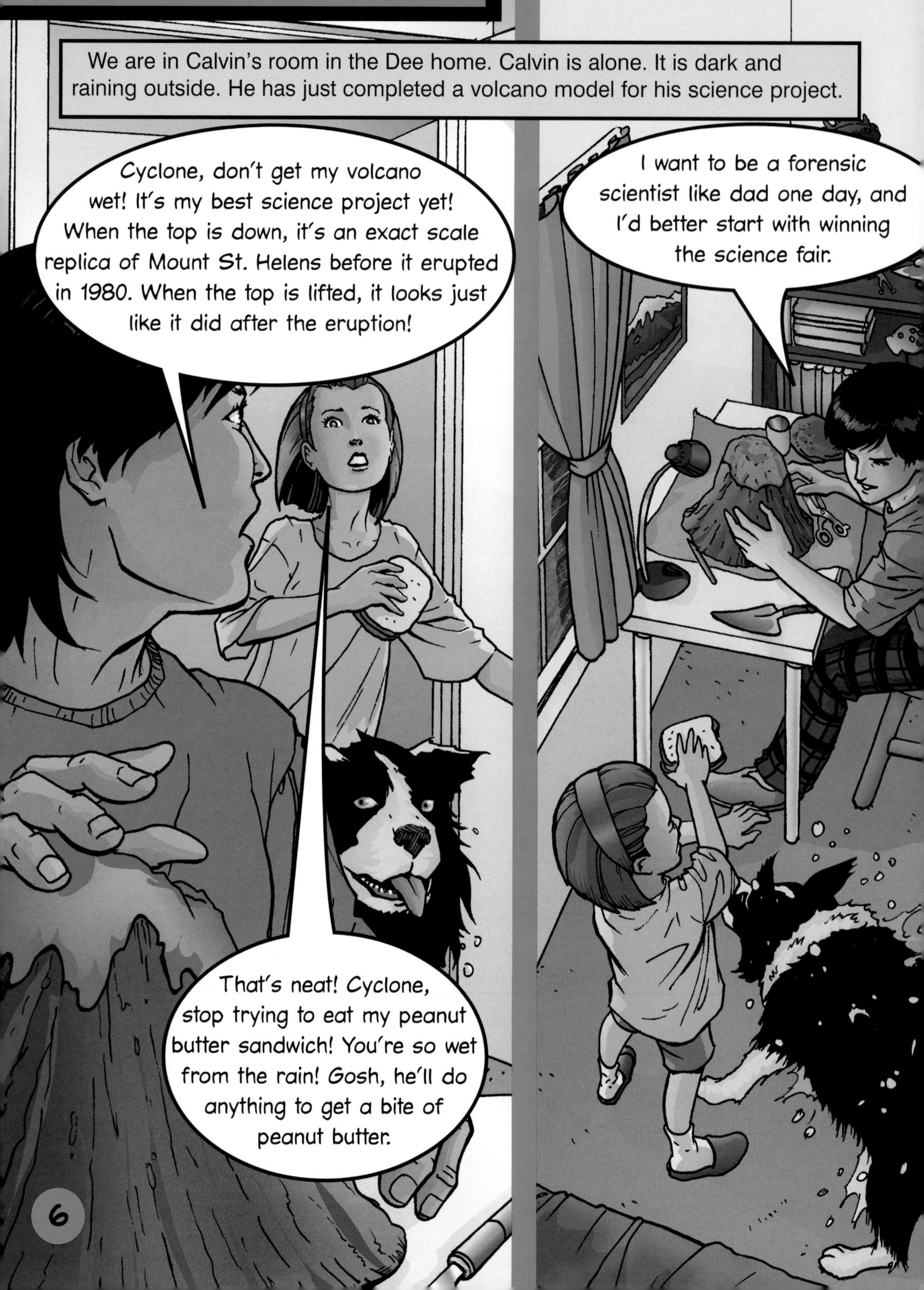
We are in Calvin's room in the Dee home. Calvin is alone. It is dark and raining outside. He has just completed a volcano model for his science project.
Cyclone, don't get my volcano wet! It's my best science project yet! When the top is down, it's an exact scale replica of Mount St. Helens before it erupted in 1980. When the top is lifted, it looks just like it did after the eruption!
That's neat! Cyclone, stop trying to eat my peanut butter sandwich! You're so wet from the rain! Gosh, he'll do anything to get a bite of peanut butter.
I want to be a forensic scientist like dad one day, and I'd better start with winning the science fair.

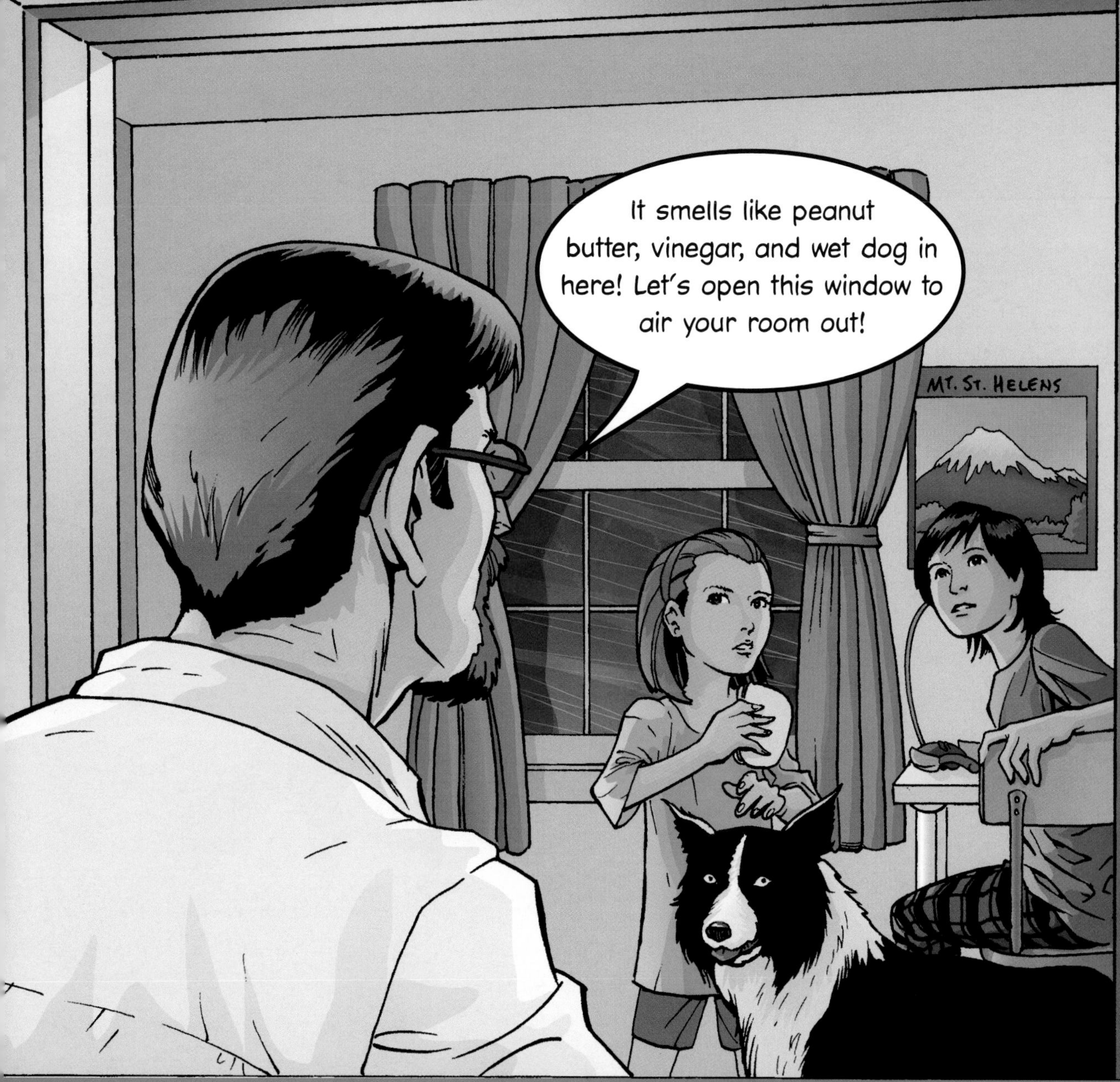
It smells like peanut butter, vinegar, and wet dog in here! Let's open this window to air your room out!
MT. ST. HELENS

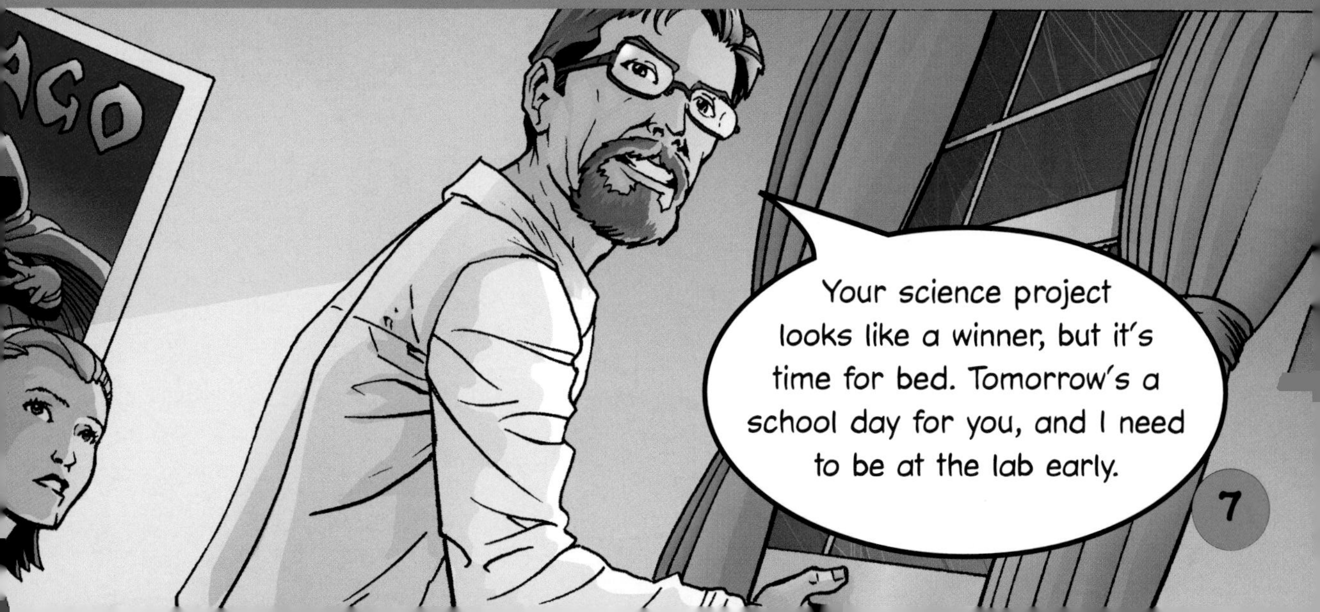
Your science project looks like a winner, but it's time for bed. Tomorrow's a school day for you, and I need to be at the lab early.

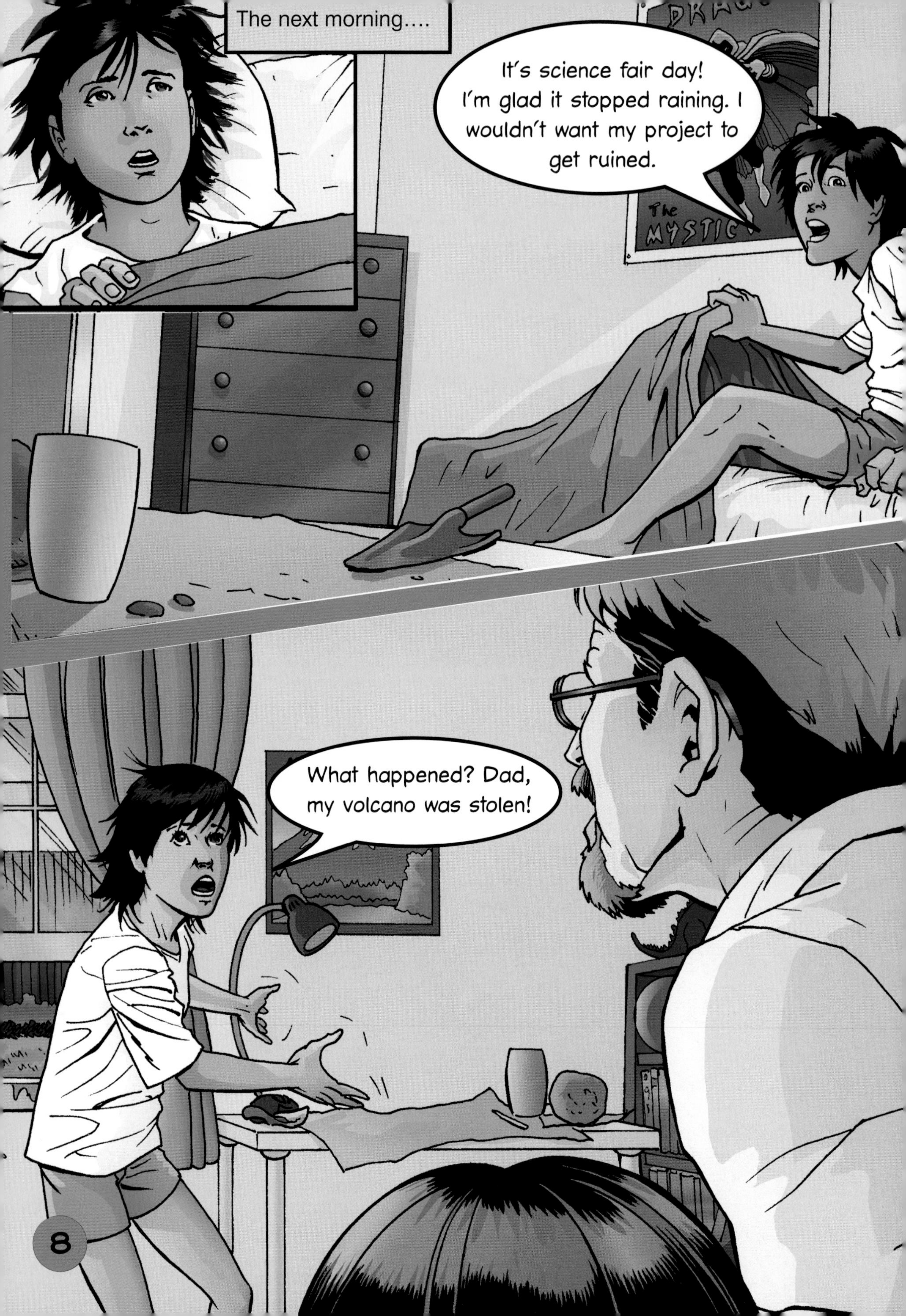
The next morning....
It's science fair day! I'm glad it stopped raining. I wouldn't want my project to get ruined.
The MYSTIC
What happened? Dad, my volcano was stolen!

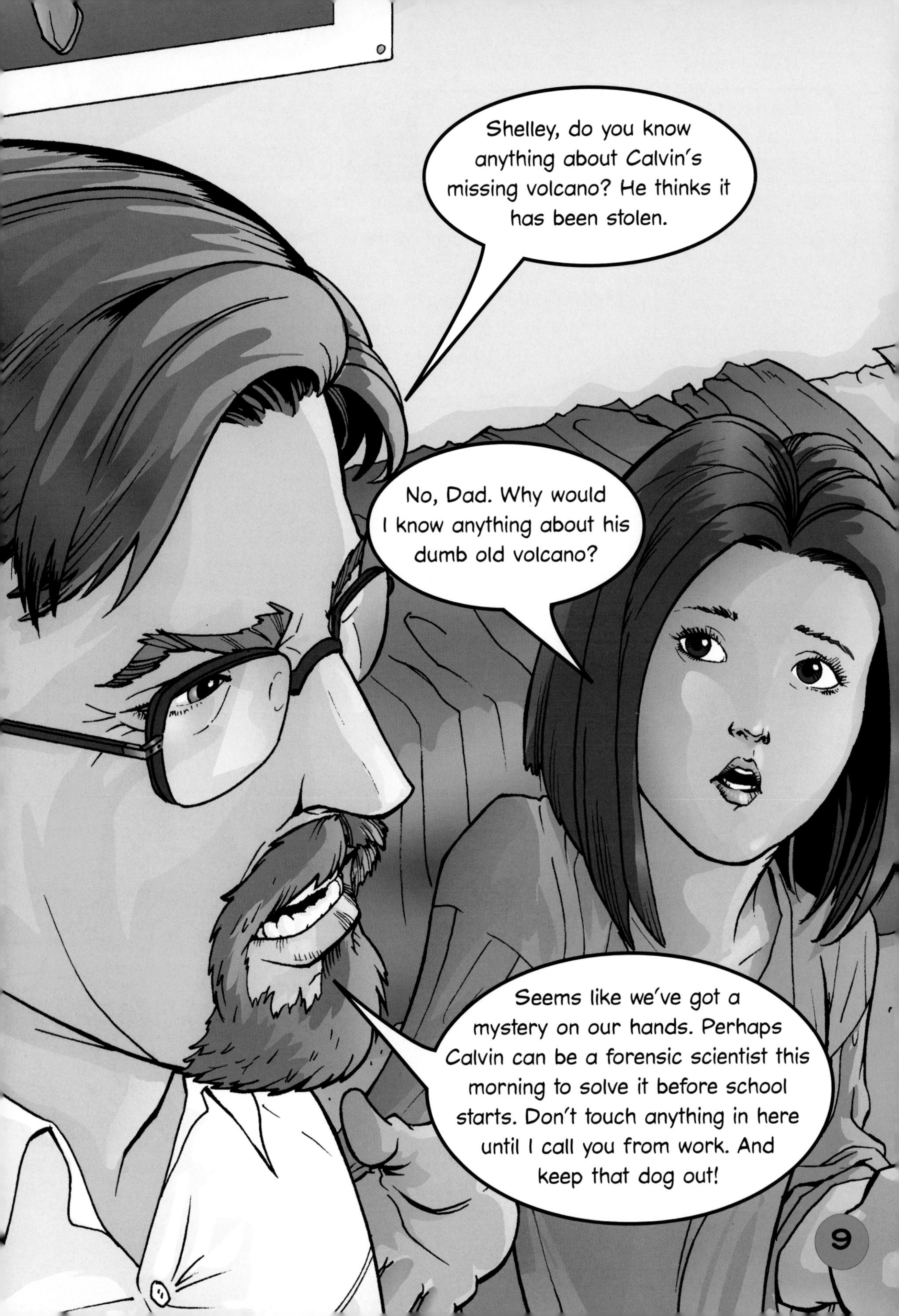
Shelley, do you know anything about Calvin's missing volcano? He thinks it has been stolen.
No, Dad. Why would I know anything about his dumb old volcano?
Seems like we've got a mystery on our hands. Perhaps Calvin can be a forensic scientist this morning to solve it before school starts. Don't touch anything in here until I call you from work. And keep that dog out!

Chapter 2: The Investigation

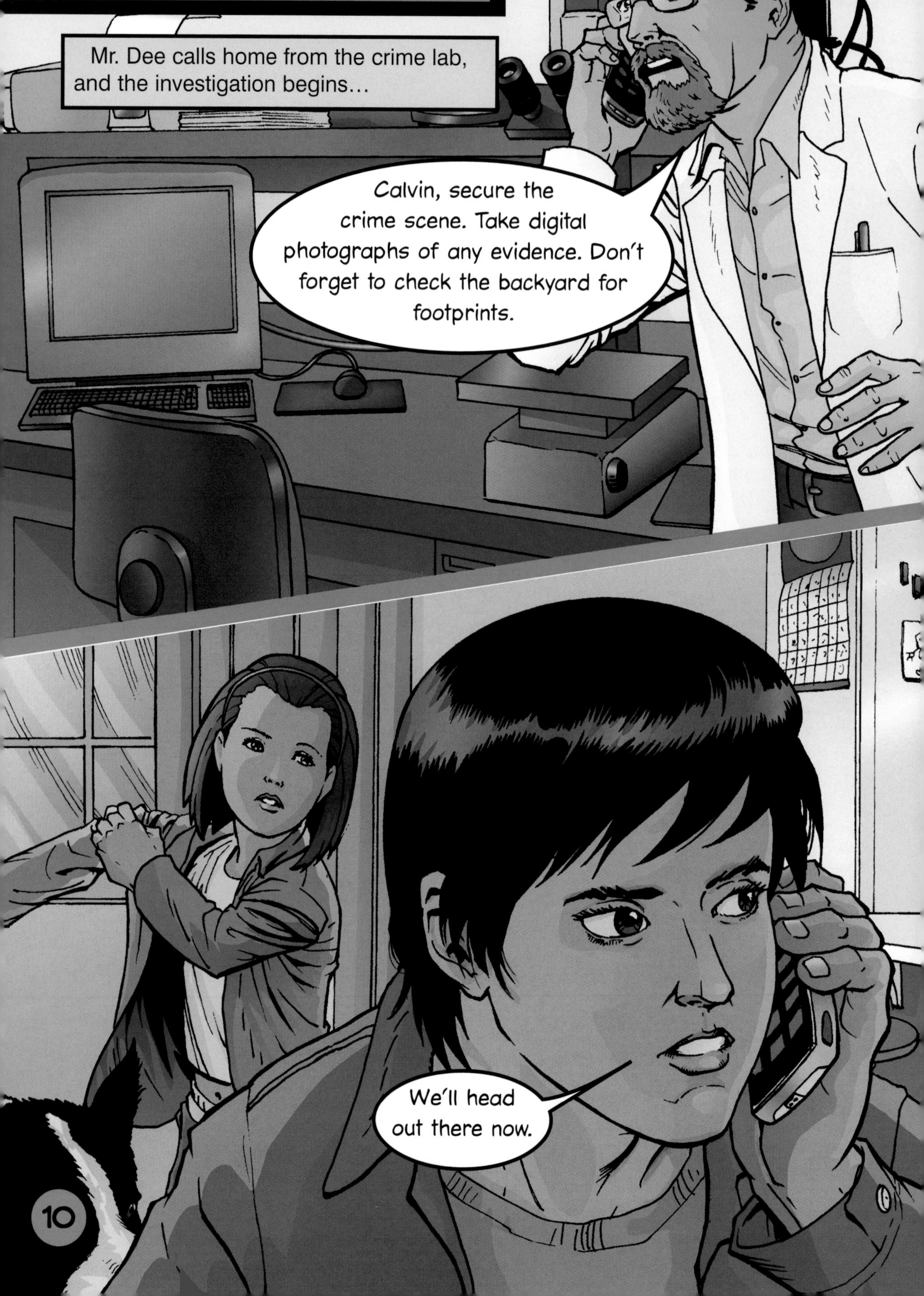
Mr. Dee calls home from the crime lab, and the investigation begins…
Calvin, secure the crime scene. Take digital photographs of any evidence. Don't forget to check the backyard for footprints.
We'll head out there now.

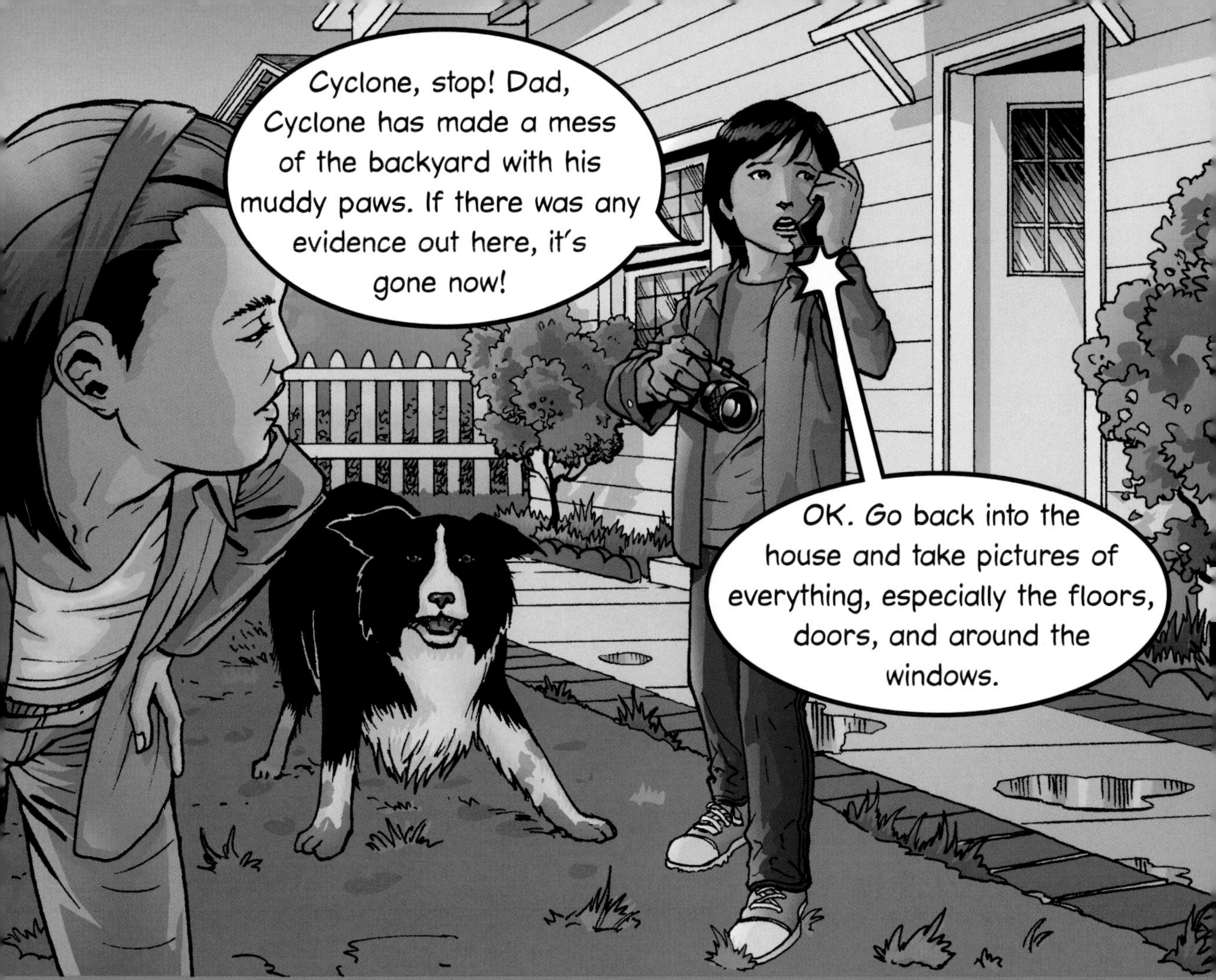
Cyclone, stop! Dad, Cyclone has made a mess of the backyard with his muddy paws. If there was any evidence out here, it's gone now!
OK. Go back into the house and take pictures of everything, especially the floors, doors, and around the windows.

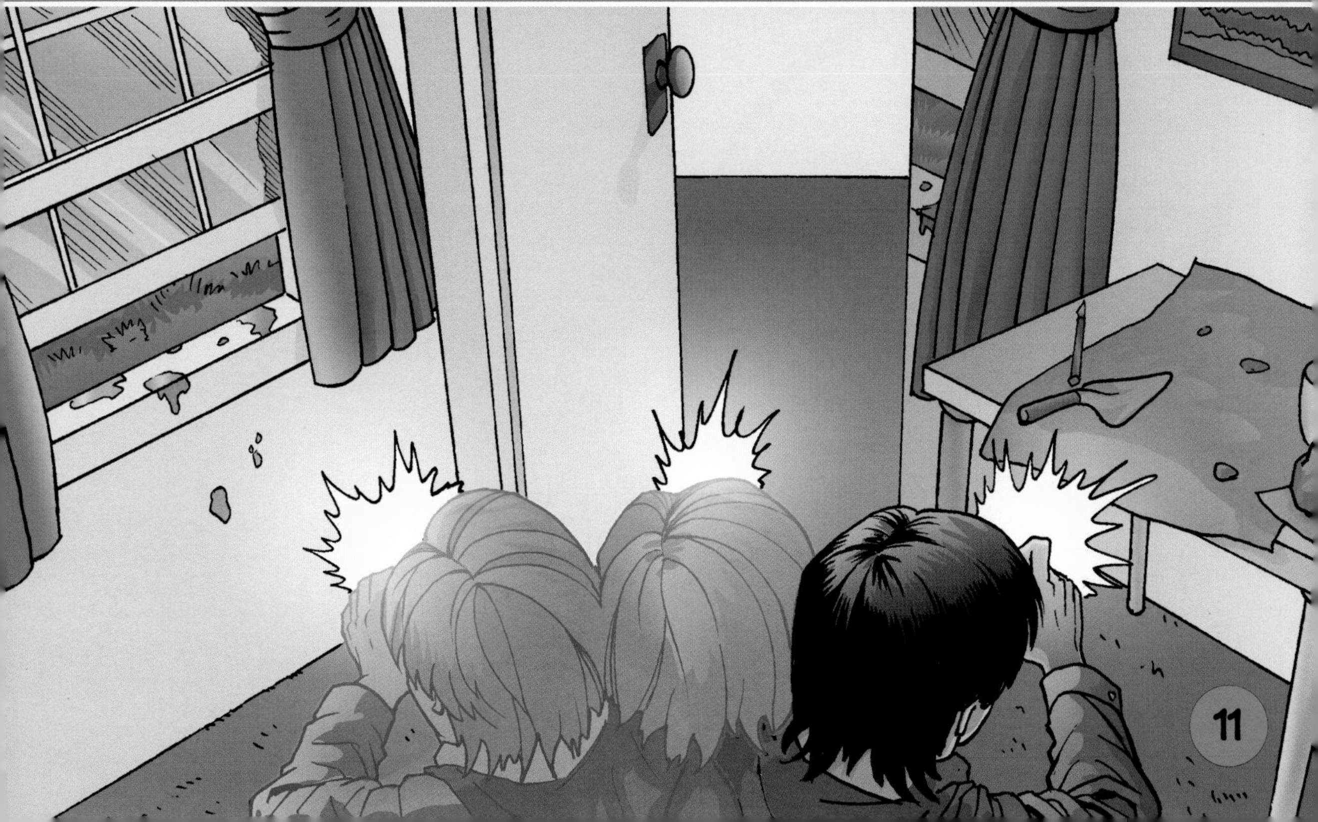

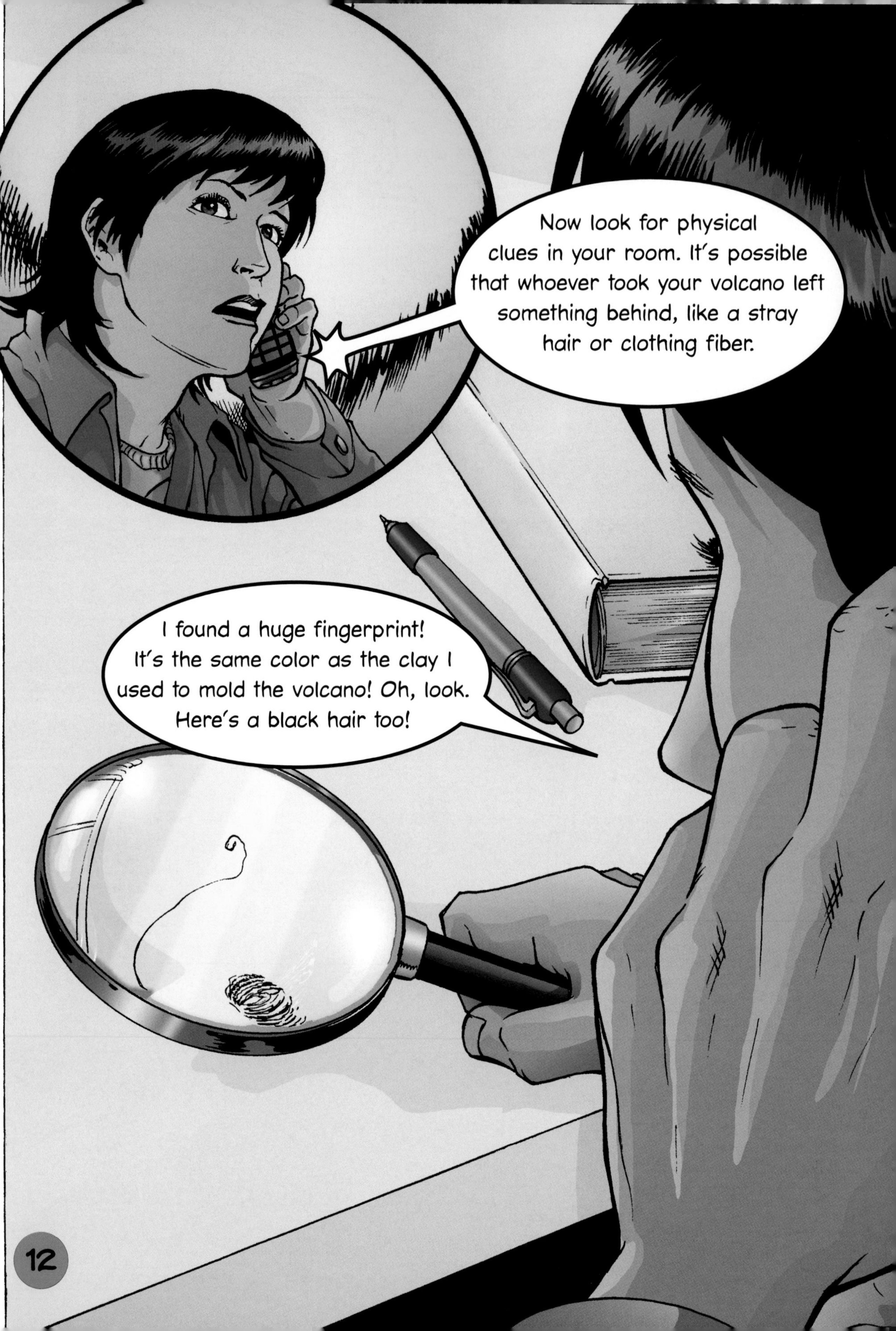
Now look for physical clues in your room. It's possible that whoever took your volcano left something behind, like a stray hair or clothing fiber.
I found a huge fingerprint! It's the same color as the clay I used to mold the volcano! Oh, look. Here's a black hair too!

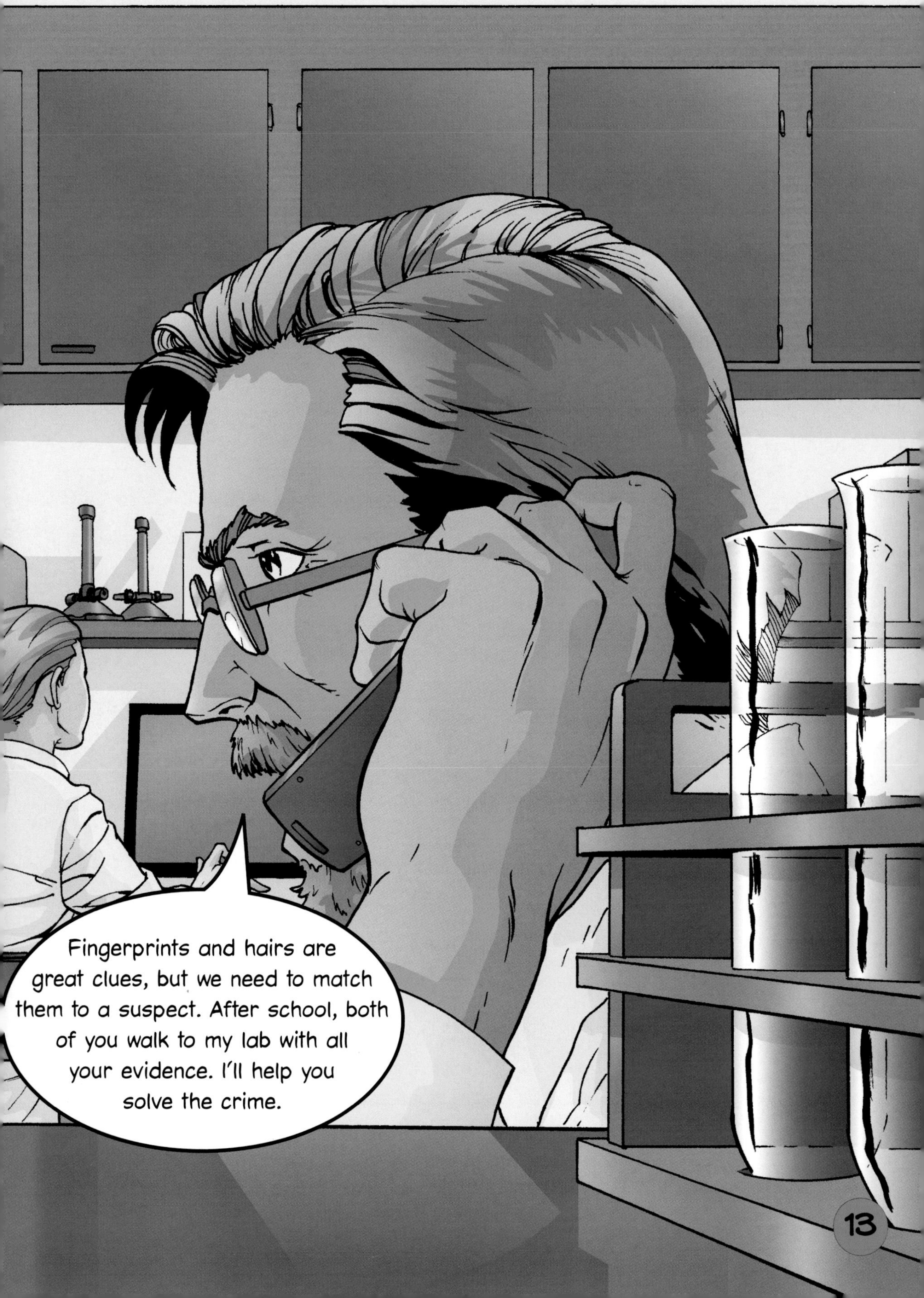
Fingerprints and hairs are great clues, but we need to match them to a suspect. After school, both of you walk to my lab with all your evidence. I'll help you solve the crime.

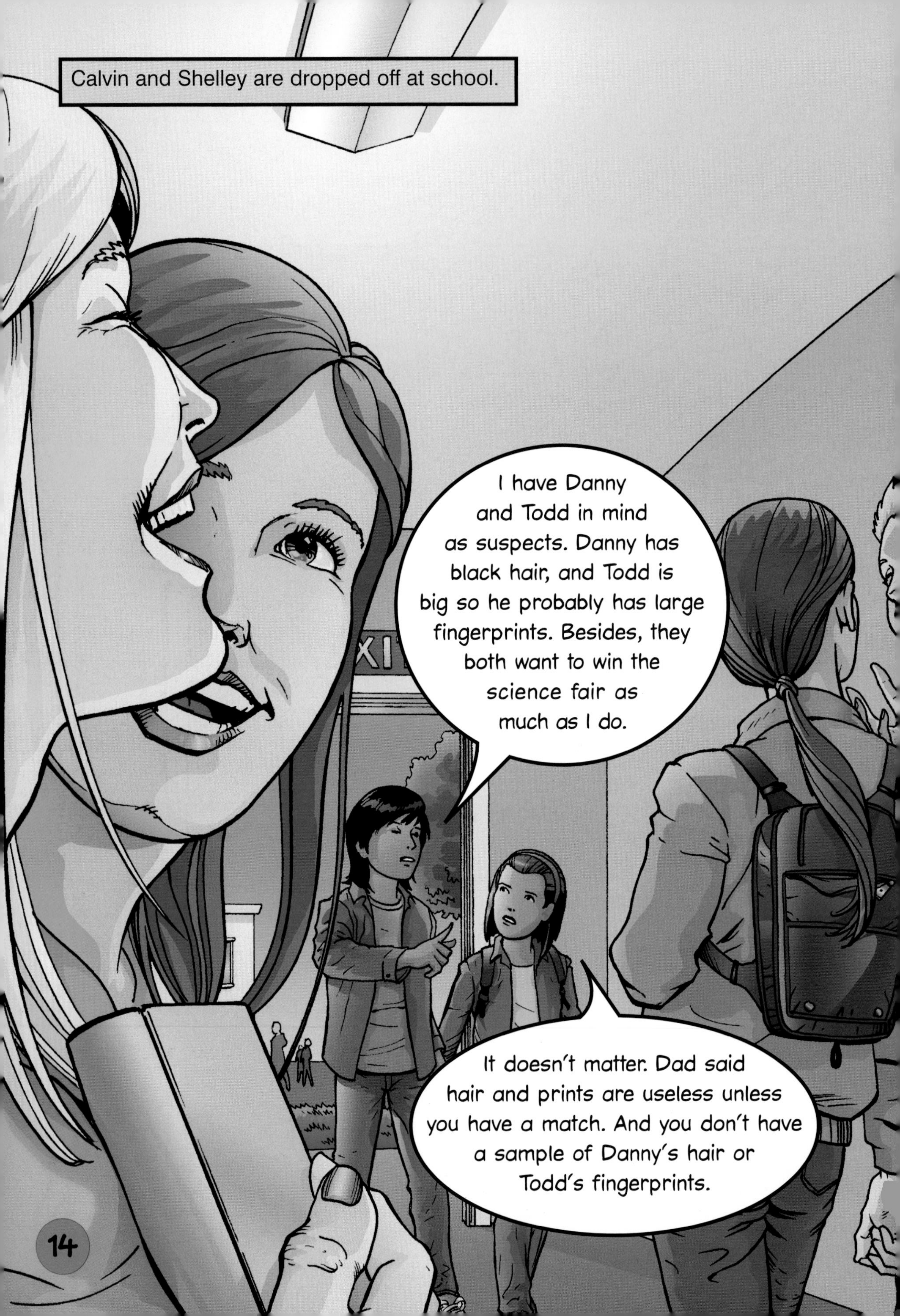
Calvin and Shelley are dropped off at school.
I have Danny and Todd in mind as suspects. Danny has black hair, and Todd is big so he probably has large fingerprints. Besides, they both want to win the science fair as much as I do.
It doesn't matter. Dad said hair and prints are useless unless you have a match. And you don't have a sample of Danny's hair or Todd's fingerprints.

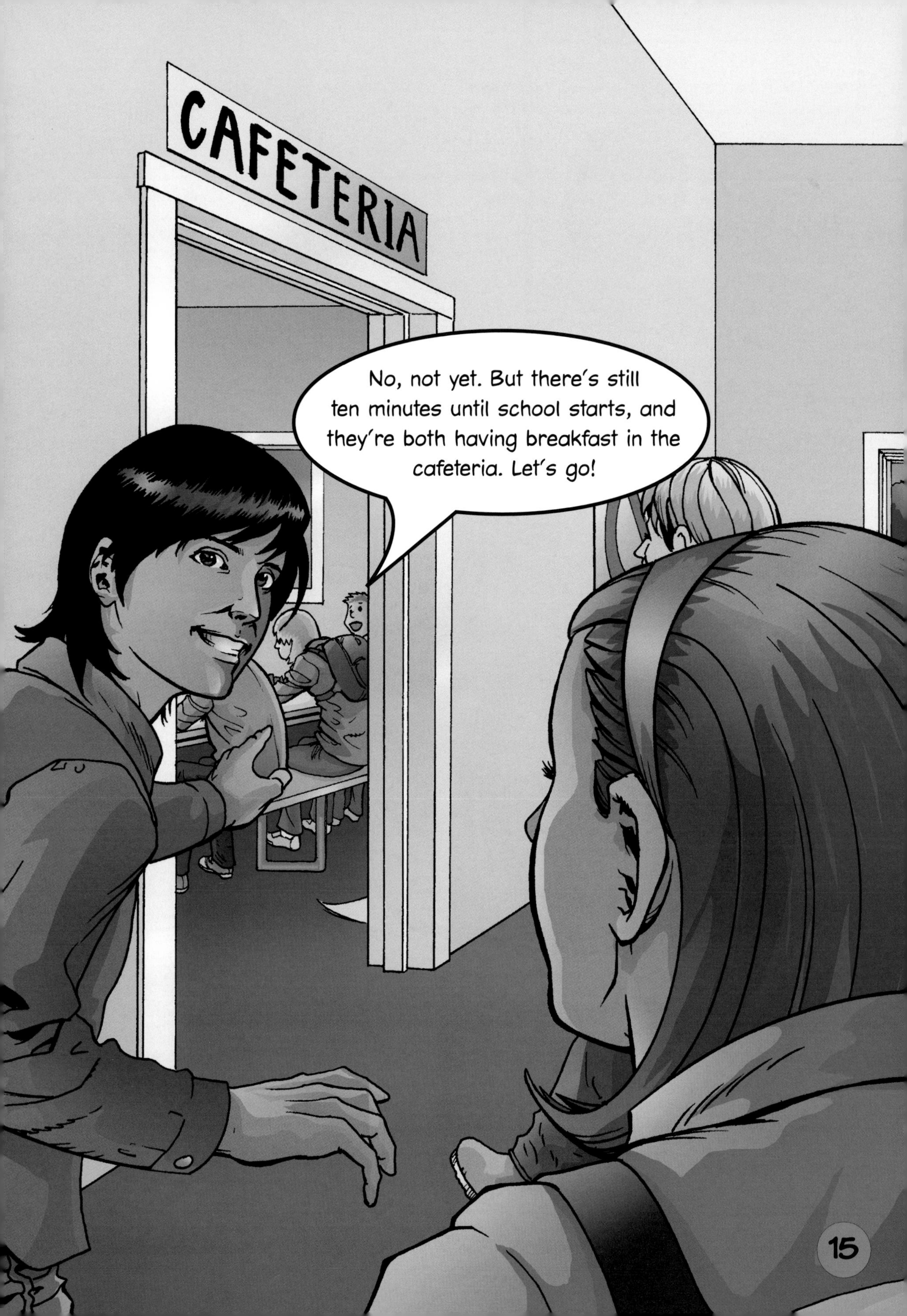
CAFETERIA
No, not yet. But there's still ten minutes until school starts, and they're both having breakfast in the cafeteria. Let's go!

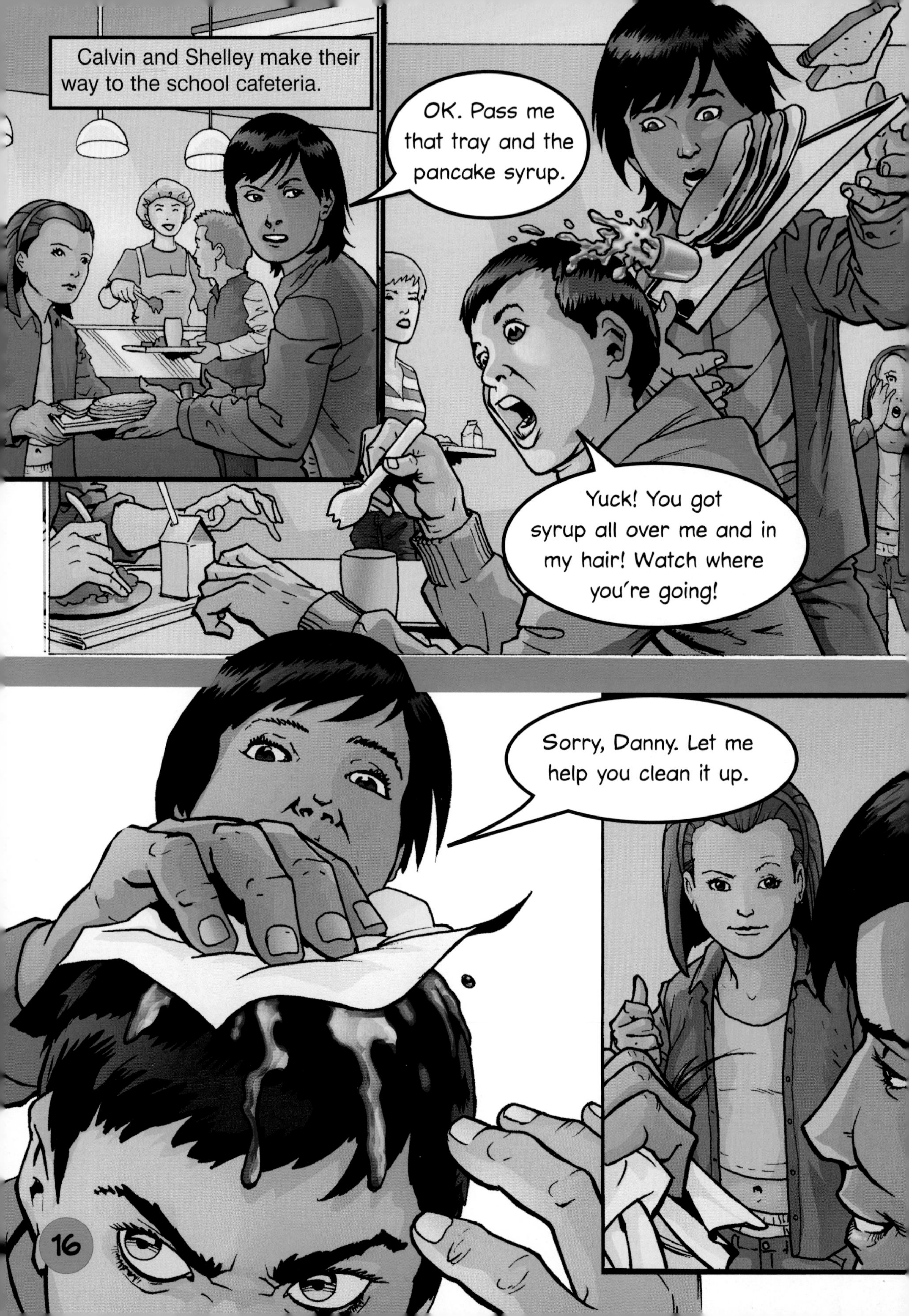

Calvin and Shelley make their way to the school cafeteria.
OK. Pass me that tray and the pancake syrup.
Yuck! You got syrup all over me and in my hair! Watch where you're going!
Sorry, Danny. Let me help you clean it up.

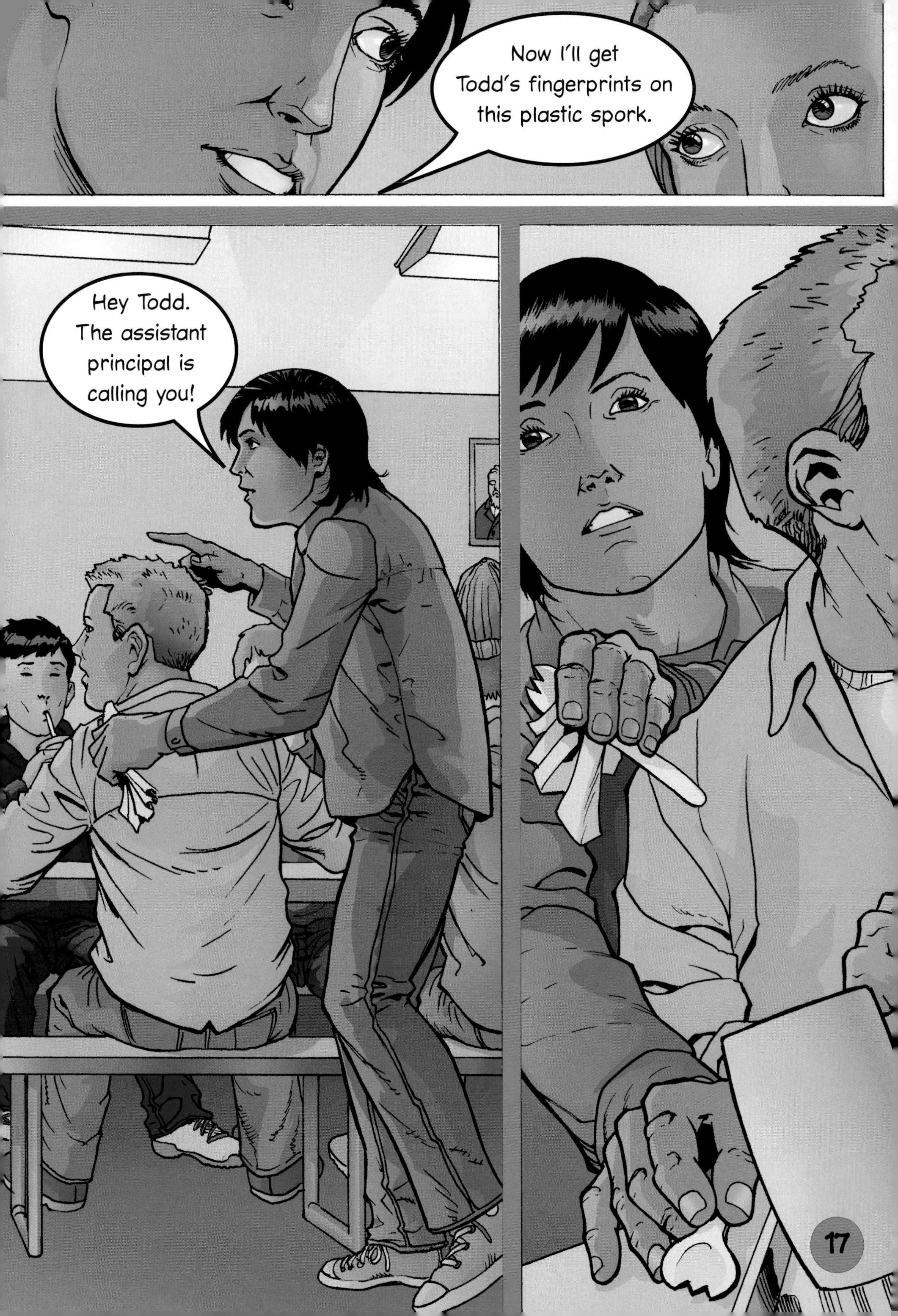
Now I'll get Todd's fingerprints on this plastic spork.
Hey Todd. The assistant principal is calling you!

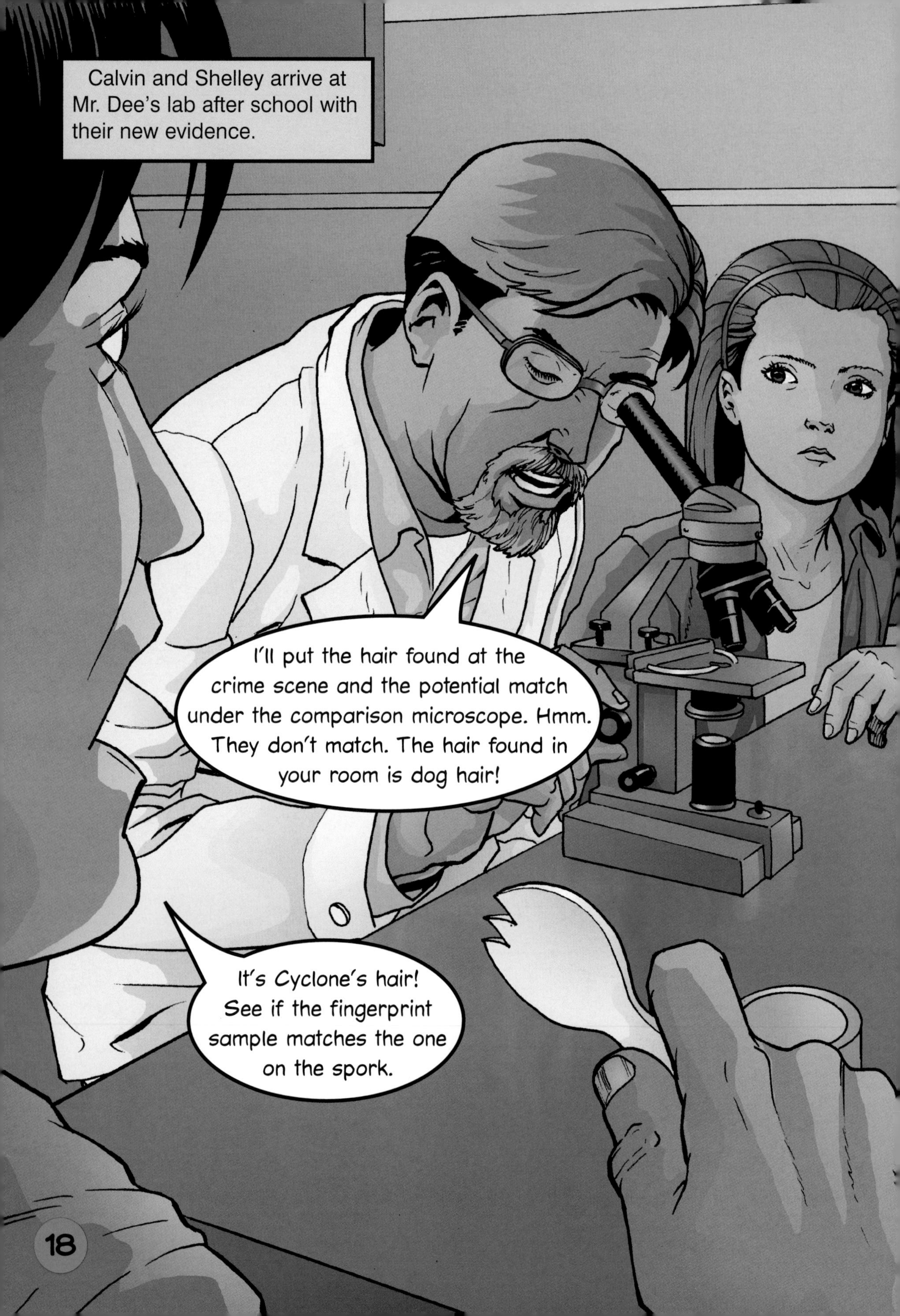
Calvin and Shelley arrive at Mr. Dee's lab after school with their new evidence.
I'll put the hair found at the crime scene and the potential match under the comparison microscope. Hmm. They don't match. The hair found in your room is dog hair!
It's Cyclone's hair! See if the fingerprint sample matches the one on the spork.

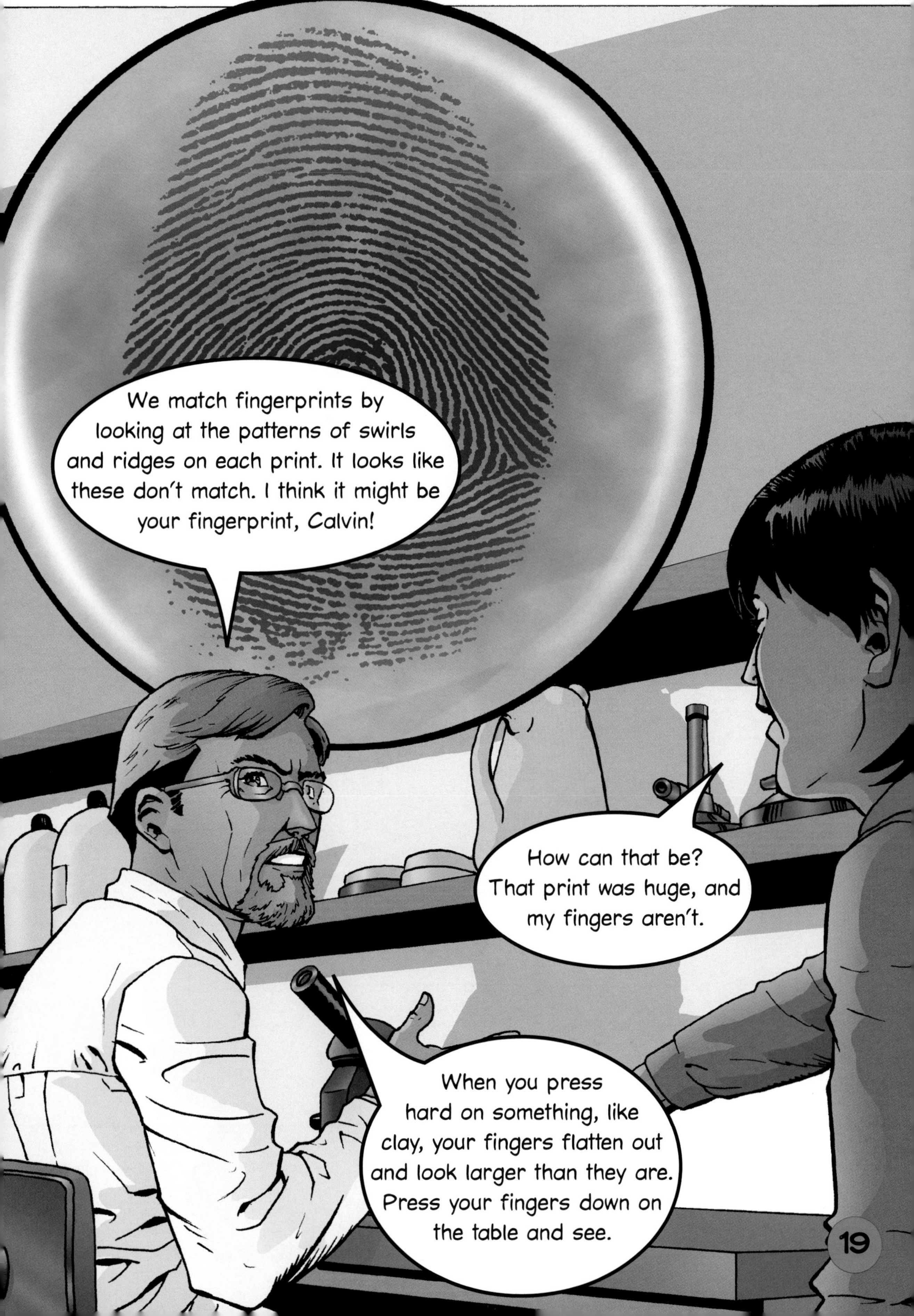
We match fingerprints by looking at the patterns of swirls and ridges on each print. It looks like these don't match. I think it might be your fingerprint, Calvin!
How can that be? That print was huge, and my fingers aren't.
When you press hard on something, like clay, your fingers flatten out and look larger than they are. Press your fingers down on the table and see.

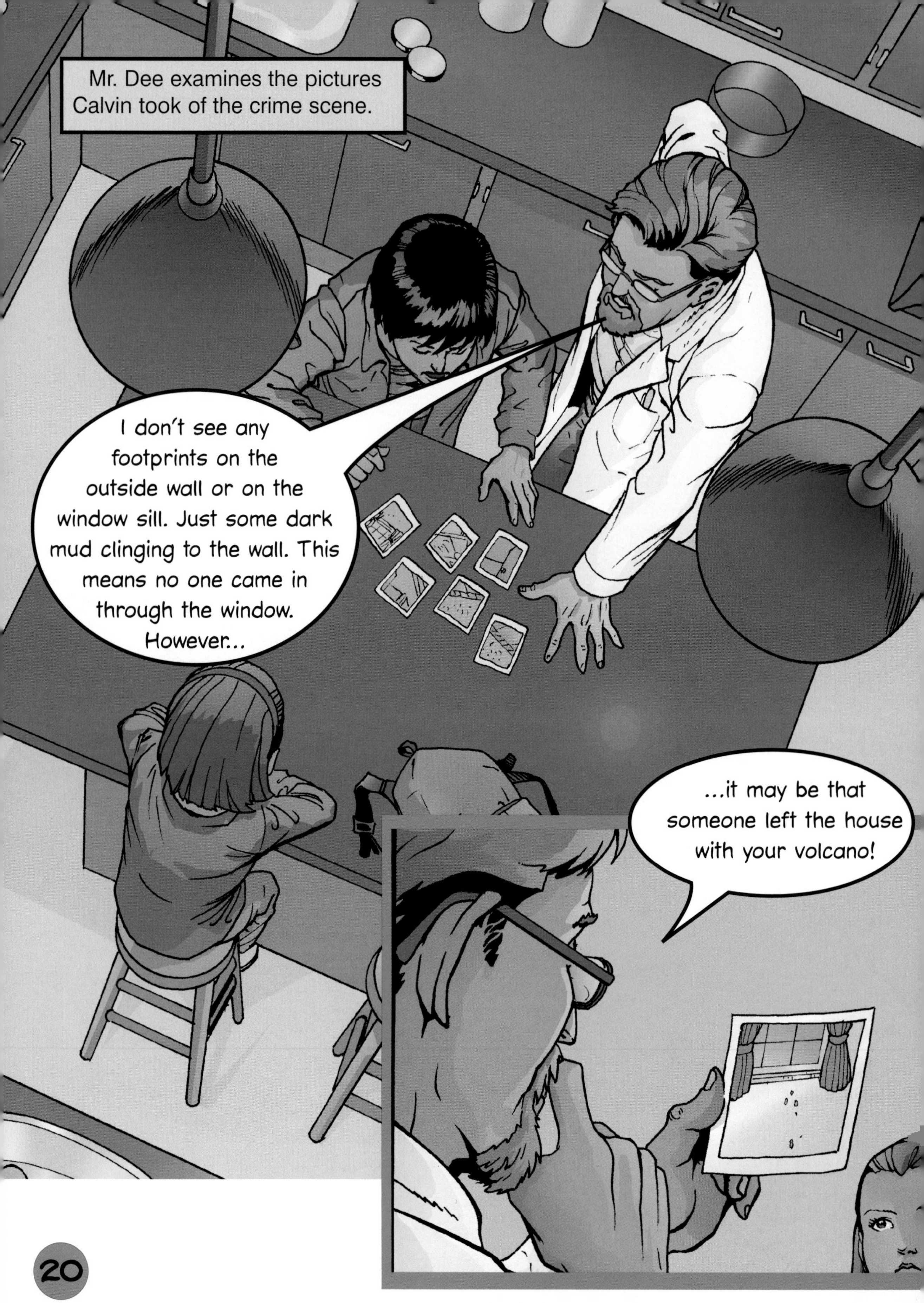
Mr. Dee examines the pictures Calvin took of the crime scene.
I don't see any footprints on the outside wall or on the window sill. Just some dark mud clinging to the wall. This means no one came in through the window. However...
...it may be that someone left the house with your volcano!

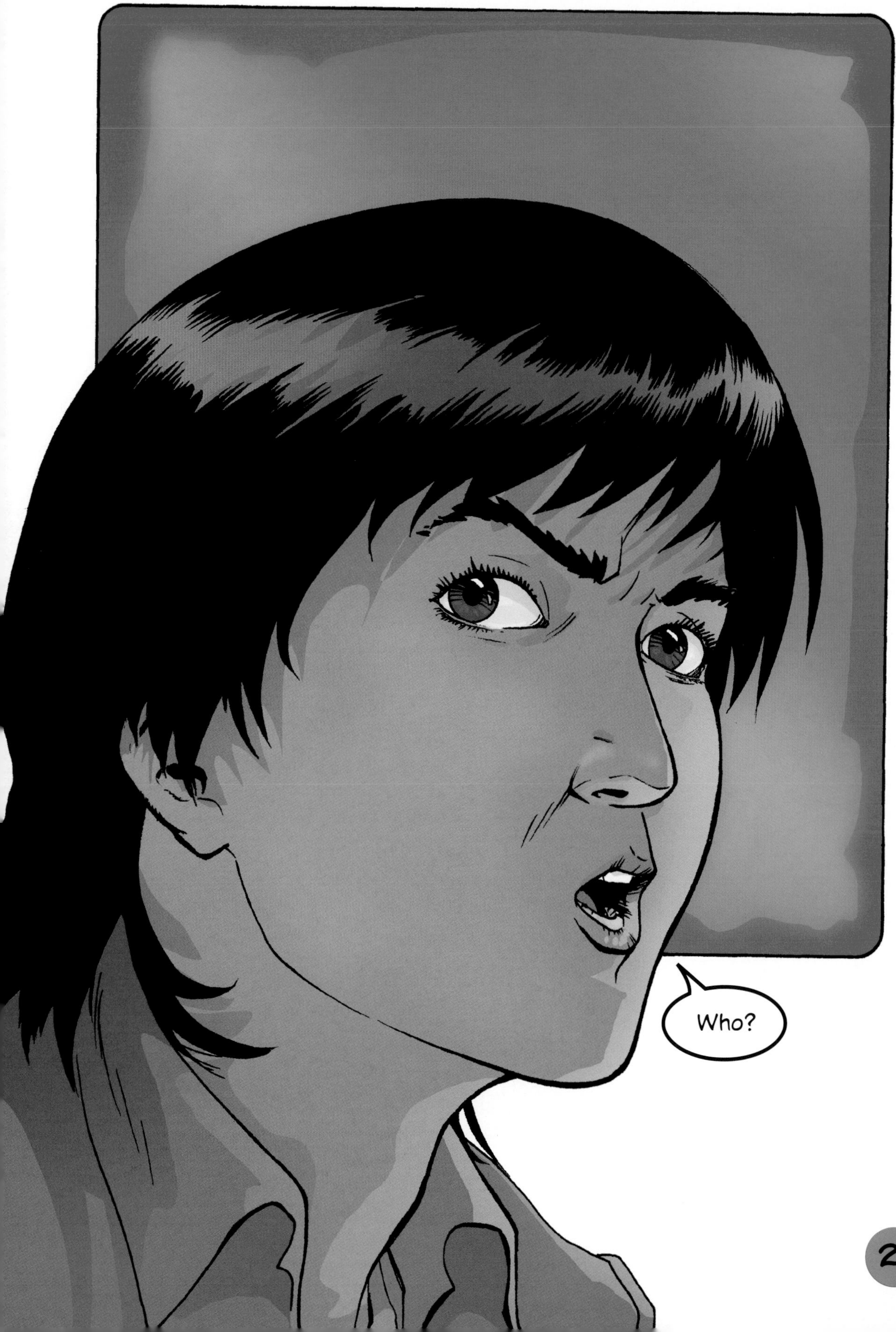
Who?

Chapter 3: The Solution

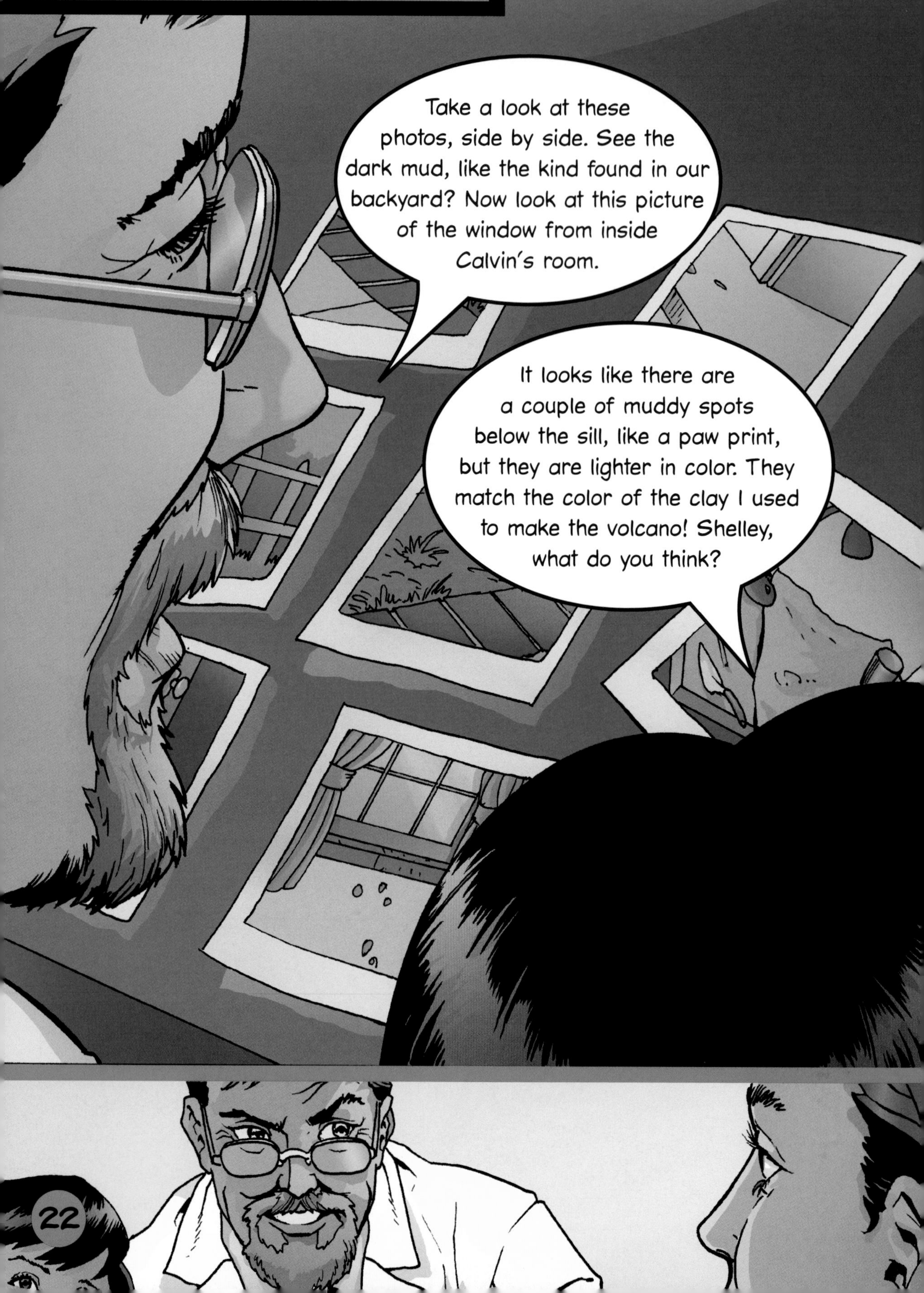
Take a look at these photos, side by side. See the dark mud, like the kind found in our backyard? Now look at this picture of the window from inside Calvin's room.
It looks like there are a couple of muddy spots below the sill, like a paw print, but they are lighter in color. They match the color of the clay I used to make the volcano! Shelley, what do you think?

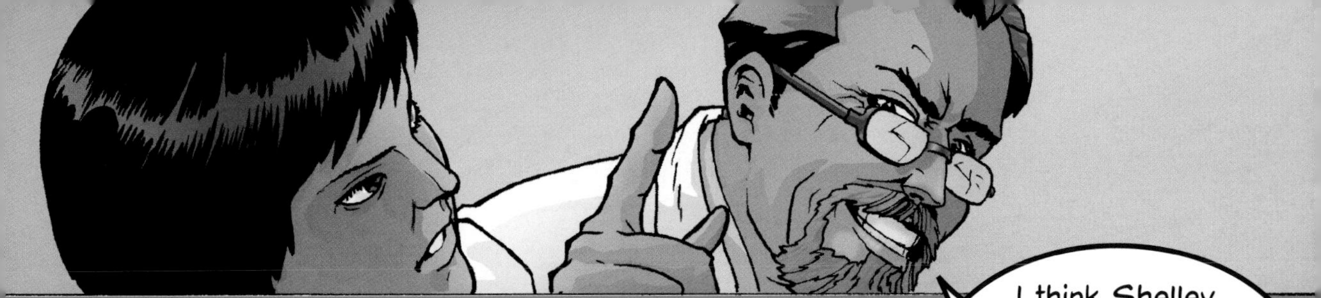

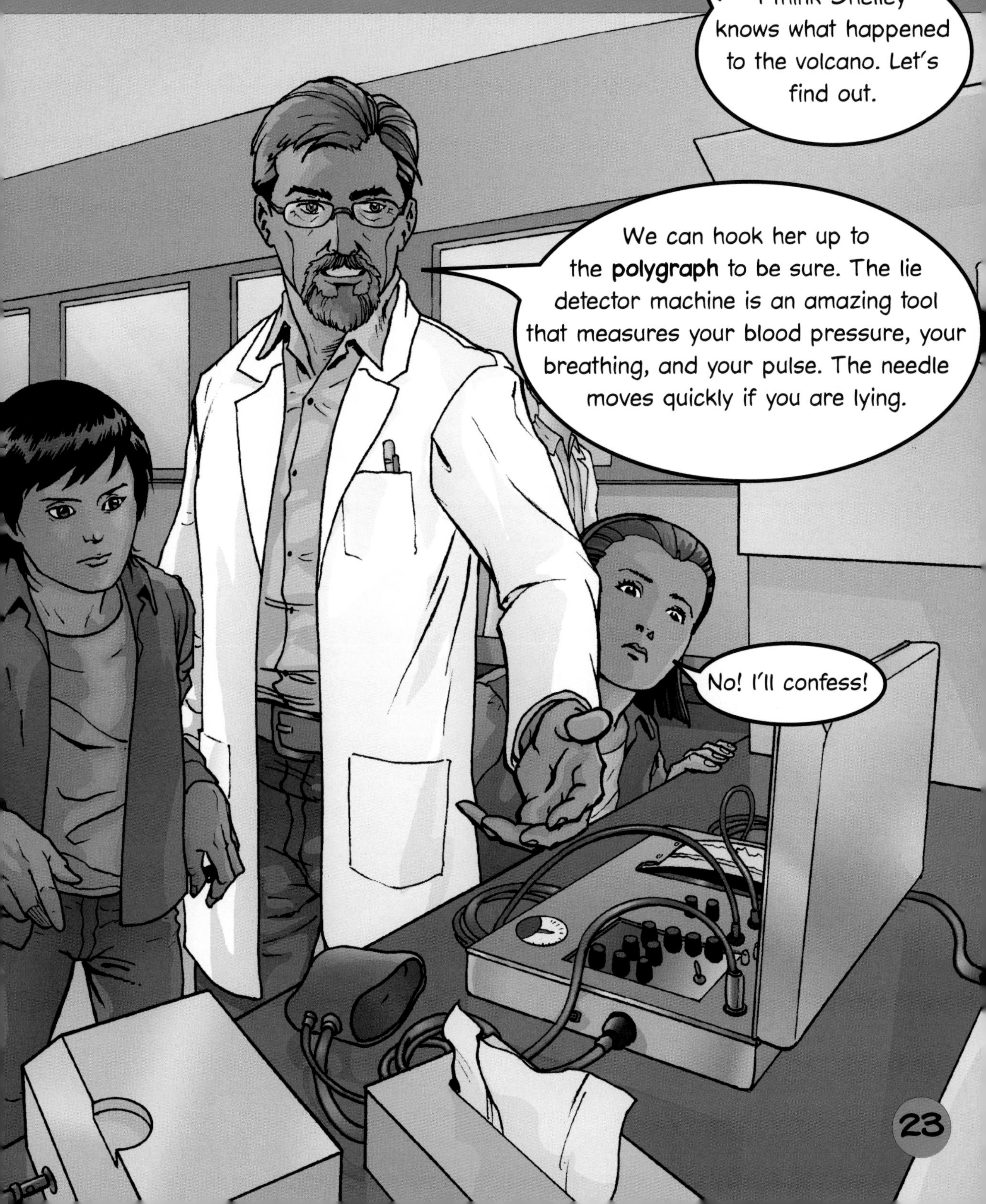
I think Shelley knows what happened to the volcano. Let's find out.
We can hook her up to the **polygraph** to be sure. The lie detector machine is an amazing tool that measures your blood pressure, your breathing, and your pulse. The needle moves quickly if you are lying.
No! I'll confess!

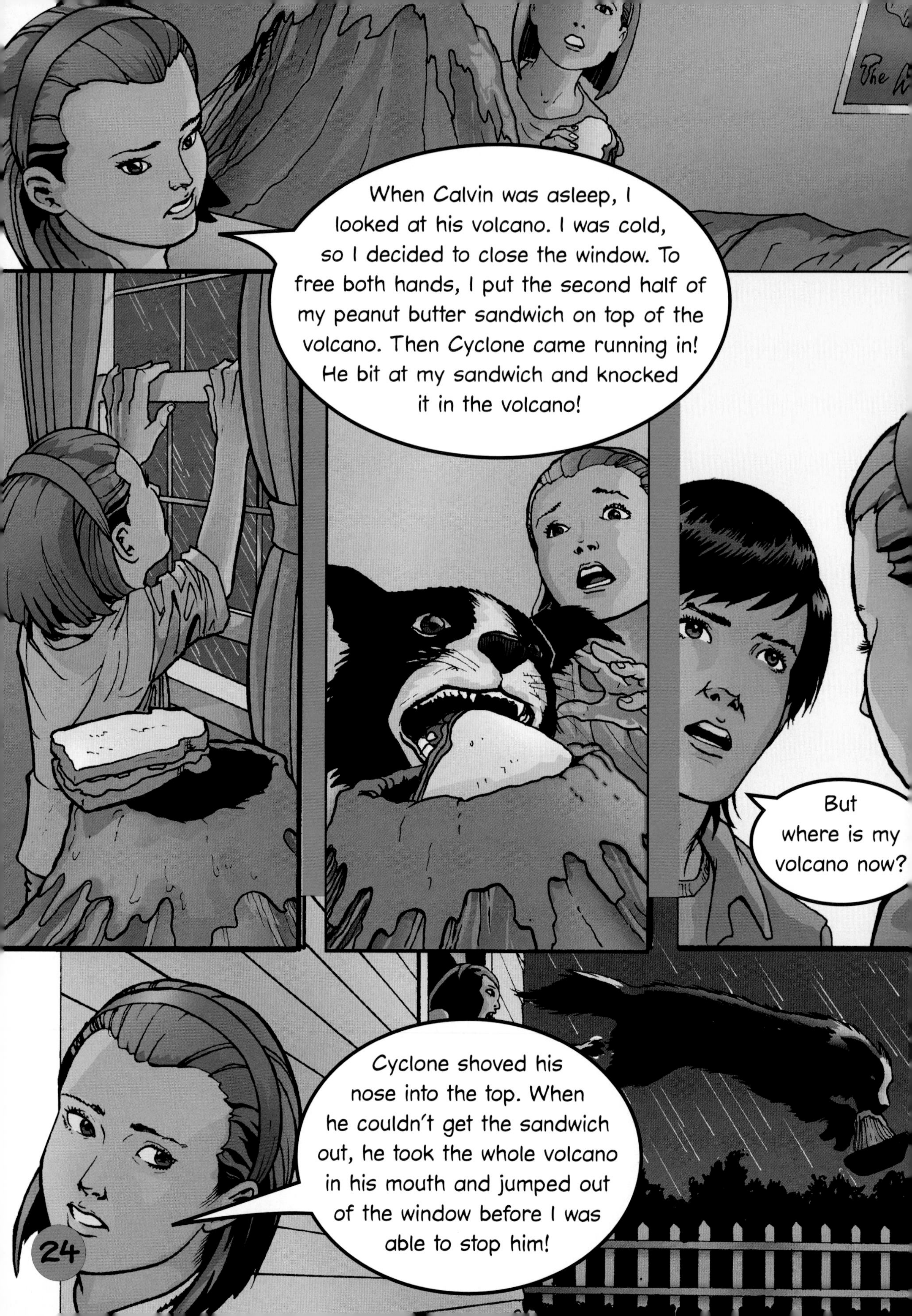
When Calvin was asleep, I looked at his volcano. I was cold, so I decided to close the window. To free both hands, I put the second half of my peanut butter sandwich on top of the volcano. Then Cyclone came running in! He bit at my sandwich and knocked it in the volcano!
But where is my volcano now?
Cyclone shoved his nose into the top. When he couldn't get the sandwich out, he took the whole volcano in his mouth and jumped out of the window before I was able to stop him!

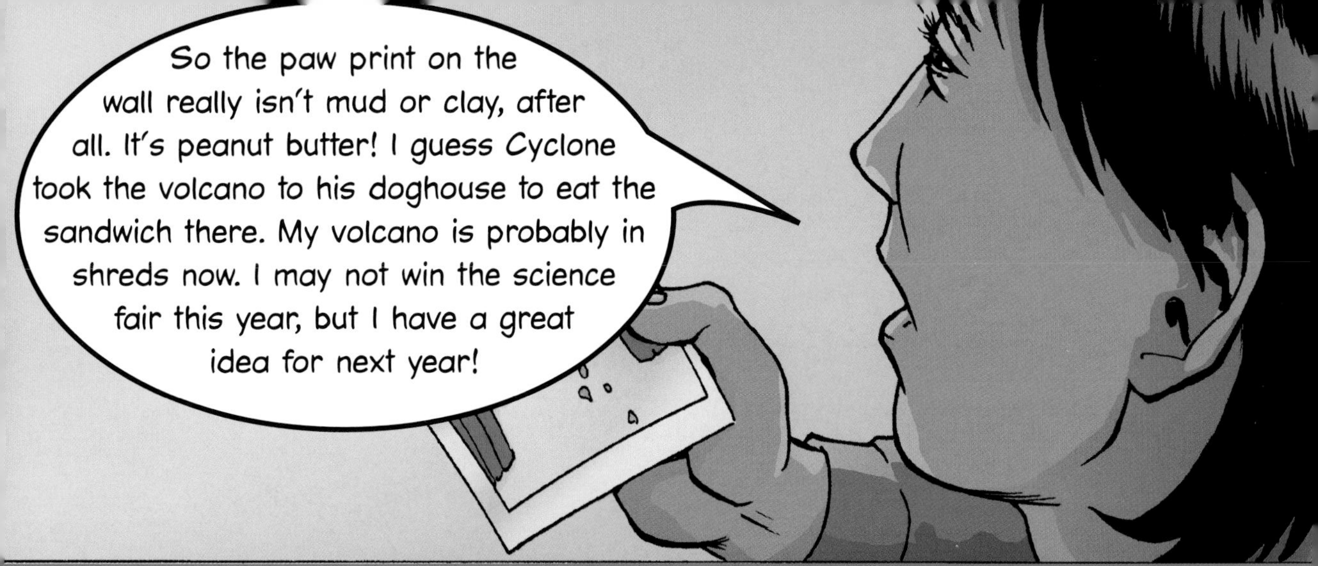
So the paw print on the wall really isn't mud or clay, after all. It's peanut butter! I guess Cyclone took the volcano to his doghouse to eat the sandwich there. My volcano is probably in shreds now. I may not win the science fair this year, but I have a great idea for next year!

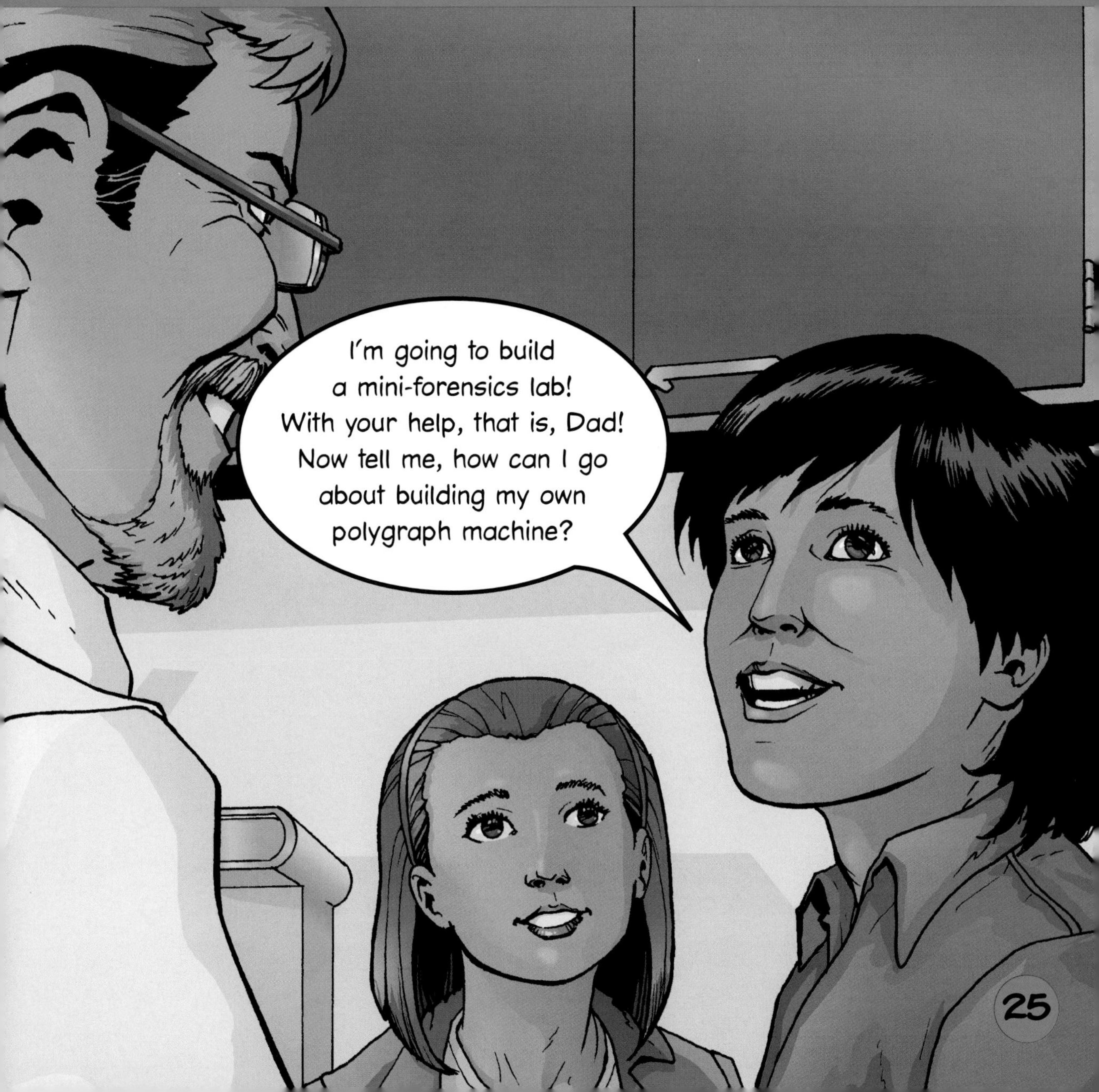
I'm going to build a mini-forensics lab! With your help, that is, Dad! Now tell me, how can I go about building my own polygraph machine?

Fields of Study in Forensics

Forensics is a huge field of study. No one can be an expert on all types of forensics. Because of this, forensic scientists often specialize in one particular field.

A forensic pathologist studies the cause of death of a person by studying the person's body. They often testify in court if someone dies as a result of a crime.

A forensic dentist helps identify a body by looking at the teeth. The first forensic dentist may have been American patriot Paul Revere. As a dentist, Revere was able to identify the body of a slain soldier in the Battle of Bunker Hill in 1775.

A fingerprint analyst specializes in identifying criminals through their fingerprints.

A ballistics expert studies the use of guns in crimes. They can identify the types of bullets used, and whether a gun has been used in more than one crime. When someone with a gun is arrested, a ballistics expert may be able to link the suspect to other crimes by examining the gun.

A forensic toxicologist studies the types of substances found in a person's body. If someone has been drugged or poisoned, the forensic toxicologist examines samples to determine whether it was the cause of death.

A document expert determines whether certain papers, such as wills, are real or not. They often study handwriting to determine who the author of a document may be.

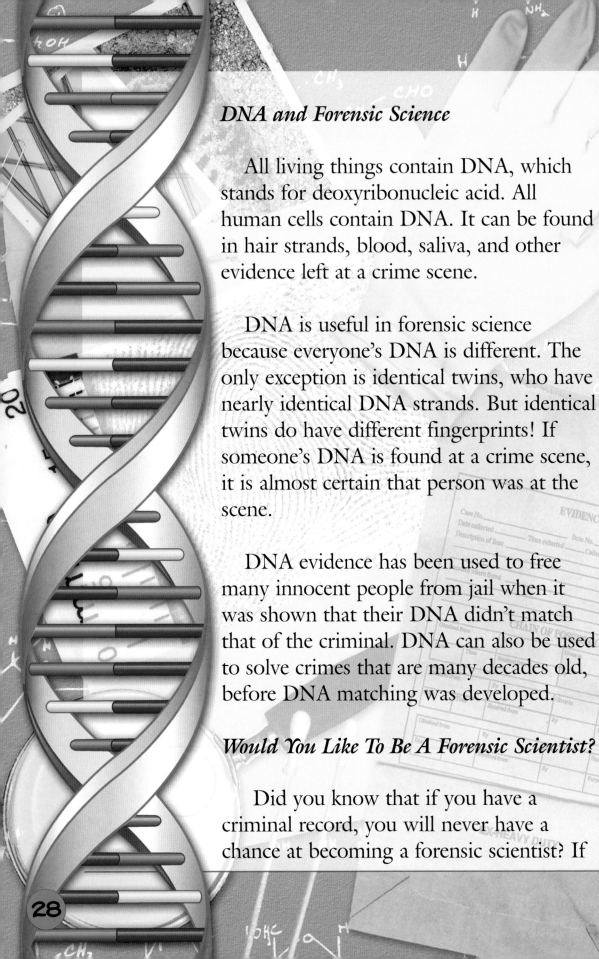

DNA and Forensic Science

All living things contain DNA, which stands for deoxyribonucleic acid. All human cells contain DNA. It can be found in hair strands, blood, saliva, and other evidence left at a crime scene.

DNA is useful in forensic science because everyone's DNA is different. The only exception is identical twins, who have nearly identical DNA strands. But identical twins do have different fingerprints! If someone's DNA is found at a crime scene, it is almost certain that person was at the scene.

DNA evidence has been used to free many innocent people from jail when it was shown that their DNA didn't match that of the criminal. DNA can also be used to solve crimes that are many decades old, before DNA matching was developed.

Would You Like To Be A Forensic Scientist?

Did you know that if you have a criminal record, you will never have a chance at becoming a forensic scientist? If you use drugs, or even smoke cigarettes in some areas, you will ruin your chances at becoming a part of this fascinating field.

Forensic science is intense and requires you to go to college and usually graduate school as well. Jobs can be hard to come by, so most universities insist that you get an undergraduate degree in an area of science. Graduate school is reserved for your area of interest in forensics.

Medical examiners have the highest paying positions, but their hours are unpredictable and requires them to deal with dead bodies on a daily basis. Crime scene examiners also have strange hours, but they usually work on location, not in an office or lab. The pay is not as high as other areas, but you are sure to be interested and challenged every day!

Websites

www.fbi.gov/kids/6th12th/investigates/investigates.htm

www.sciencenewsforkids.org/articles/20041215/Feature1.asp

www.fbi.gov/hq/cjisd/takingfps.html

pbskids.org/dragonflytv//show/forensics.html

Glossary

clues (KLOOS): Concrete samples or known facts that help you find the answers to a question or a mystery.

comparison (com-PAHR-iss-uhn): A comparison shows how things are alike and different.

evidence (EV-uh-duhnss): Evidence is information collected that helps to prove the truth of something.

forensics (fuh-REN-siks): Forensics involves the use of science to help investigate and solve crimes.

investigation (in-vess-tuh-GAY-shuhn): In an investigation, a scientist tries to find out as much as possible about a subject, such as a crime.

lab (LAHB): A lab, or laboratory, is a special room with equipment that helps a scientist run experiments.

polygraph (POL-ee-graf): This is a special machine that measures body functions to determine if a person is telling the truth when questioned. It is also known as a lie detector machine.

secure (si-KYOOR): To secure something is to make something safe, especially by closing it tightly.

soil (SOYL): Plants grow in soil. It is also called dirt.

suspect (SUH-spekt): A suspect is someone thought to be responsible for a crime.

Index

blood pressure 23
clues 12, 13
comparison microscope 18
crime scene 10, 18, 20, 28
evidence 10, 11, 13, 18, 20, 28
erupted 6
fiber 12
footprints 10, 20
forensic(s) 4, 6, 9, 25, 26

forensic scientist 4, 6, 9, 26, 27, 28
lab 7, 10, 13, 18, 25
lie detector 23
Mount St. Helens 6
polygraph 23, 25
pulse 23
replica 6
ridges 19
sample(s) 14, 18, 27
soil 10
swirls 19

About the Author

Tim Clifford is an education writer and the author of many nonfiction children's books. He has two wonderful daughters and two energetic Border Collies that he adopted from a shelter. Tim became a vegetarian because of his love for animals. He is also a computer nut and a sports fanatic. He lives and works in New York City as a public school teacher.

About the Artists

Ken Hooper has been a professional artist since 1985 when he embarked on a career in comics. His list of comic art include Swamp Thing, Aquaman, Star Trek, Indiana Jones, Elfquest, and Primal Force, to name a few.

Lance Borde earned his degree in English and Fine Arts through the university system in his home state of California. His career includes work in the arts and in graphics and design.